OhS

# table toppers

27 Projects for Stylish Living

Jean & Valori Wells

C&T PUBLISHING

Text © 2007 Jean Wells and Valori Wells

Artwork © 2007 C&T Publishing, Inc.

Publisher: Amy Marson

Editorial Director: Gailen Runge

Acquisitions Editor: Jan Grigsby

Editor: Candie Frankel

Technical Editors: Elin Thomas, Wendy Mathson, and Teresa Stroin

Copyeditor: Wordfirm Inc.

Proofreader: Stacy Chamness

Cover Designer: Kristy K. Zacharias

Design Director/Book Designer: Kristy K. Zacharias

Illustrator: John Heisch and Kirstie L. Pettersen

Production Coordinators: Tim Manibusan and Kerry Graham

Photography: Diane Pedersen and Luke Mulks, unless otherwise noted

Published by C&T Publishing, Inc., P.O. Box 1456, Lafayette, CA 94549

Front cover: Asian print tablecloth, inset trim placemats, and napkins

Back cover: Striped Table Runner, Inset-Trim Placemat, Runner-Inset

Tablecloth, Side Panels Placemat

All rights reserved. No part of this work covered by the copyright hereon may be used in any form or reproduced by any means—graphic, electronic, or mechanical, including photocopying, recording, taping, or information storage and retrieval systems—without the written permission of the publisher. The copyrights on individual artworks are retained by the artists as noted in *Oh Sew Easy Table Toppers*. These designs may be used to make items only for personal use or donation to nonprofit groups for sale. Each piece of finished merchandise for sale must carry a conspicuous label with the following information: Designs © 2007 Jean Wells and Valori Wells from the book *Oh Sew Easy Table Toppers* from C&T Publishing.

Attention Copy Shops: Please note the following exception—publisher and author give permission to photocopy page 29 for personal use only.

Attention Teachers: C&T Publishing, Inc., encourages you to use this book as a text for teaching. Contact us at 800-284-1114 or www.ctpub.com for more information about the C&T Teachers' Program.

We take great care to ensure that the information included in our books is accurate and presented in good faith, but no warranty is provided nor are results guaranteed. Having no control over the choices of materials or procedures used, neither the author nor C&T Publishing, Inc., shall have any liability to any person or entity with respect to any loss or damage caused directly or indirectly by the information contained in this book. For your convenience, we post an up-to-date listing of corrections on our website (www.ctpub.com). If a correction is not already noted, please contact our customer service department at ctinfo@ctpub.com or at P.O. Box 1456, Lafayette, CA 94549.

Trademark (™) and registered trademark (®) names are used throughout this book. Rather than use the symbols with every occurrence of a trademark or registered trademark name, we are using the names only in the editorial fashion and to the benefit of the owner, with no intention of infringement.

Library of Congress Cataloging-in-Publication Data

Wells, Jean

  Oh sew easy table toppers : 27 projects for stylish living / Jean and

Valori Wells.

    p. cm.

  Includes index.

  ISBN-13: 978-1-57120-359-5 (paper trade : alk. paper)

  ISBN-10: 1-57120-359-1 (paper trade : alk. paper)

  1. Household linens. 2. Table setting and decoration. 3. Machine sewing.

  I. Wells, Valori. II. Title.

  TT387.W473 2007

  746.9'6--dc22

          2006023348

Printed in China

10 9 8 7 6 5 4 3 2

## Acknowledgments

*Oh Sew Easy Table Toppers* was a very creative book for us to style. Our desire to showcase a variety of styles led us once again to The Wild Hare, a home accessories store managed by Carolyn Spencer. We borrowed props from the store and raided our own stash of items to come up with stylish settings for our projects. Carolyn offered invaluable help and guidance every step of the way. Thank you to Andrea Storton and Janet Storton for the use of their dining rooms for set shots. Once again, we extend our gratitude to Luke Mulks, our photographer, for a fabulous job. His knowledge of photographic lighting and his understanding of how the photos would be presented in the book kept us on target.

The members of the editorial and design team for the Oh Sew Easy series have come together once again to produce *Table Toppers*: Candie Franke as editor, Elin Thomas as technical editor, and Kristy K. Zacharias as designer. Thank you most of all to C&T Publishing for believing in our series of soft-furnishings books.

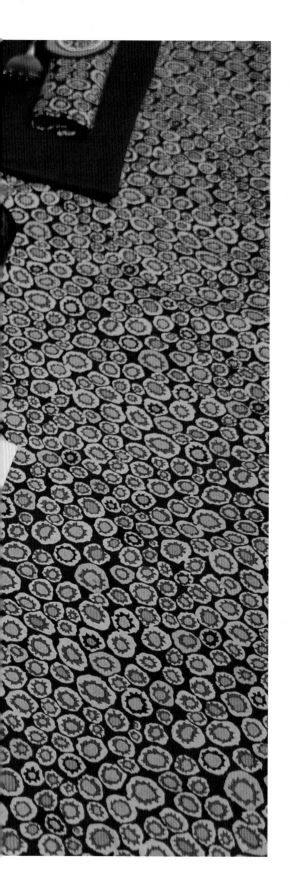

# contents

# Introduction

Table toppers are a wonderful way to create a decorative, inviting mood for dining at home. Whether you are hosting a holiday dinner party or just rounding up the family for spaghetti on a Wednesday night, a well-dressed table sets the mood for fun and conversation.

Sewing your own table toppers is an easy, affordable way to infuse your dining space with personality. Placemats extend a cheery welcome at the breakfast table, especially if family members have different morning routines and tend to eat in shifts. For lunch or supper, swap in a tablecloth and flowers or candles and you've instantly changed the dining ambiance from short-order grill to chic little downtown café.

In *Oh Sew Easy Table Toppers*, we show you how to sew a collection of table furnishings that you can mix and match. Included are placemats, tablecloths, runners, and square center-pieces. We especially like the layered look—for example, layering placemats on top of a tablecloth and adding coordinating napkins—to dress up the table and enhance the dining experience. You'll also learn how to factor in other accessories, such as your dinnerware and flatware, to achieve a coordinated look. We enjoy "shopping" for design ideas in home accessories catalogs and magazines, and we encourage you to do the same.

With the success of *Oh Sew Easy Pillows* and *Oh Sew Easy Duvet Covers & Curtains*, we are more committed than ever to bringing you fresh, easy-to-sew designs that will make your home unique and stylish. The abundant fabric prints and colors available to today's home sewer are guaranteed to set your creative juices flowing. Tropical prints, Asian motifs, and stripes are just a few of the fabrics we used to create our table toppers; we had great fun discovering ways to use clever novelty prints related to cooking, food, and the kitchen. Our approach, as always, is to teach you the basics and provide clear, concise project recipes so that you can sew creatively and with confidence.

Happy sewing—and happy dining!

Jean & Valori

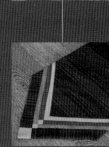

# what's on the menu?

The colors, patterns, and textures of the table ensemble color every dining experience. A beautifully set table sets the mood and makes everyone feel welcome and special.

A leafy print placemat sets off a celadon plate, a glass tumbler, and a bud vase on a single-serving snack tray. A mint green napkin adds a refreshing accent.

# Placemats

Placemats are simple to make and easy to use. They dress up a table and add instant color, without getting too formal or fussy. Before choosing a fabric for placemats, think about the dishes that will go on them. The colors and styles should coordinate and set off one another. Concentrate on the total ensemble, rather than on achieving an exact color match. When we were shopping for plates for the dining room shown on our cover, our first impulse was to match the brick red color in the fabric exactly. When we found a set of bright red plates, we were totally amazed at the energy and excitement they brought to the table.

Our placemat designs are rectangular and in two sizes: 12″ × 18″ and 14″ × 18″. Choose the smaller size for luncheon plates or snacks, the larger size for dinner plates. You will still have ample room for a folded napkin and flatware. Each of our placemat recipes makes a set of two placemats. To make placemats for four, six, or eight settings, multiply the fabric yardage by two, three, or four, respectively.

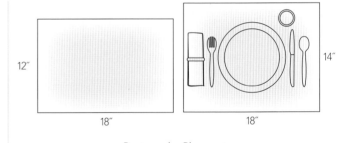

Rectangular Placemats

You can easily apply our sewing techniques to make placemats in other shapes, such as a square or an oval. To us, a 14″ × 14″ square placemat suggests European or Asian style. Placemats you already own can make perfect templates. Simply trace around the shape and then draw a second line ¼″ beyond the traced outline for the seam allowance.

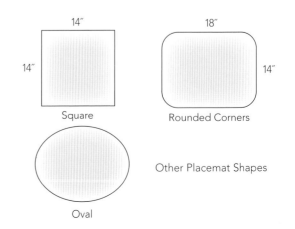

Square

Rounded Corners

Other Placemat Shapes

Oval

Cabbage leaf luncheon plates look right at home on a vegetable print tablecloth. The whimsical centerpiece announces the arrival of fresh spring produce.

# Tablecloths

Tablecloths are always appropriate, whether you are setting the table for a holiday meal or enjoying an impromptu picnic on the lawn. With our quilting background, it's no wonder we enjoy layering placemats and runners on top of the tablecloth in our table settings and trying out different color combinations. For a picnic cloth, we like bright, casual prints.

Tablecloths can be made in various shapes and sizes. The smallest commercially available size, 54″ × 54″, is called a breakfast cloth. This versatile covering will work on round, oblong, or square tables. It is especially eye-catching when placed at an angle. We have sewn an even smaller square, about 40″ × 40″, using 42″- to 44″-wide cotton quilting fabric.

The beautiful fabric patterns and colors available to quilters are just too enticing to resist for our home decor projects.

Typical sizes for commercially made rectangular tablecloths are 70″ × 90″, 70″ × 108″, and 70″ × 126″. Round tablecloths are usually 70″ or 90″ in diameter. Oval tablecloths are also available. The extra-wide fabrics that are specially milled for commercial use are not marketed to the home sewer. To achieve a 70″ width in our home-sewn tablecloths, we use various seaming techniques to join two or more pieces of fabric. Sometimes the seams are camouflaged, and other times they become an integral part of the design. Making tablecloths gives us yet one more reason to indulge our passion for mixing and matching quilting fabrics.

# tablecloth shapes and sizes

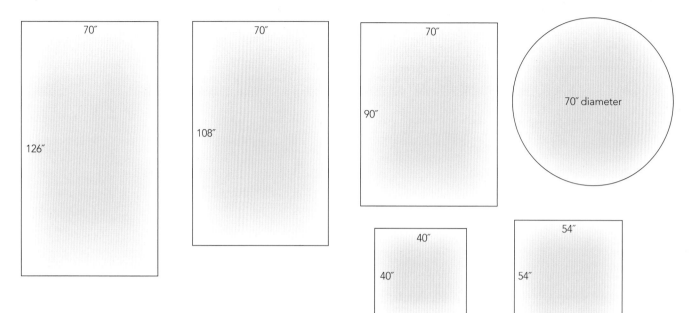

70″
126″

70″
108″

70″
90″

70″ diameter

40″
40″

54″
54″

When you sew your own tablecloths, you have the option of customizing the size to fit your table. Measure the length and width (or diameter) of the table top. To determine the drop, or length of fabric that overhangs the edge of the table top, pull up a dining chair to the table and sit down in the chair. Use a tape measure to measure from the top edge of the table to your lap, or a little above it. We personally don't like a lot of fabric from a tablecloth sitting in our laps. Add the drop measurement around the edges to determine your custom tablecloth size. You can use the same technique to custom-size a round tablecloth that drops to the floor.

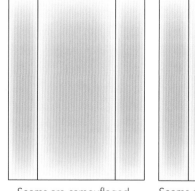

Seams are camouflaged.　　　Seams are part of the design.

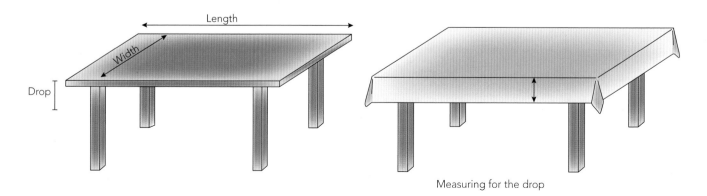

Length

Width

Drop

Measuring for the drop

A glazed ceramic jug, brimming with yarrow from the garden, inspired the earthy fabric palette for our Tuscan table runner.

# Table Runners

Table runners are for the most part decorative. They "run" down the center of the table, either as stand-alone pieces or to anchor other decorative objects. Between meals, a runner and a bowl of fruit or a vase of flowers can dress up a bare table. For a quick family meal, just add a placemat at every setting.

We like to layer runners on top of our tablecloths to add a punch of color. A small collection of runners in different holiday themes and colors can carry you through a whole year of celebrations. On a buffet table or sideboard, a runner can unify the presentation and also protect your furniture. Our table runner designs are full of surprises. Shapes run from simple rectangles to rectangles with tapered ends and decorative strip piecing.

For pleasing proportions, the width of the runner should be about one-third the width of the table. For example, if your table is 48″ wide, a good runner width would be about 16″. Note that this measurement allows an ample 16″ on either side of the runner for placemats and individual table settings. The length of the runner is variable. A runner can sit on top of the table, or it can hang off the ends of the table. There is no right or wrong; the length you choose should reflect your table, the setting, and the look you want. You can easily alter the width or length of the runners in our recipes to make a custom fit for your table.

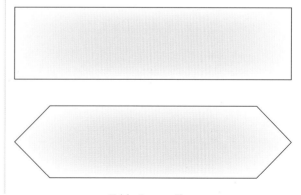

Table Runner Shapes

A table mat lets you enjoy, rather than conceal, a handsome wood table. The saturated colors and floral print of this mat bring a touch of Provence to the dining nook.

Sitting down to eat with family and friends is one of life's pleasures. When you sew table linens yourself, you'll be able to choose from a wide selection of fabric patterns and colors. You'll be able to build a personal household collection of table toppers to mix and match in different combinations—all for an affordable price.

## Table Mats

A table mat is placed in the center of the table. Bigger than a placemat, a table mat can be square, round, or rectangular. The shape we prefer is a square turned on point, so that each diner sees it as a diamond. Like a table runner, a mat is the perfect landing pad for a vase of flowers, a candle, or a bowl of fruit to brighten a table between meals.

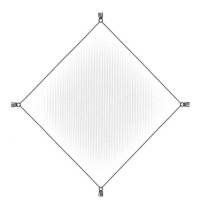

Table Mat With Tassels

Sew napkins in a solid color to accent printed placemats.

# Napkins

Napkins are more than just a necessity for polite dining. Think of napkins as a decorative detail on the table. Sewing your own napkins lets you add just the right touch of color or pattern to round out your dining ensemble.

A standard napkin size, good for lunches and light suppers, is 18″ × 18″. For special occasions and holidays, you might opt for a more generous 20″ × 20″ or 22″ × 22″ napkin. Our recipes include several edge and corner treatments so that you can add a professional touch to your table linens down to the last detail. We also include some designs for sewing your own napkin rings.

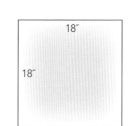

Napkin Sizes

Red, plum, and green are the recurring color families in this layered dining ensemble. Muted shades work to keep the bolder colors under control. Plants and candles on the table are part of the color scheme and reflect the Asian simplicity of the design.

# Choosing Fabrics

Printed and solid cotton quilting fabrics are appropriate for all of our table topper projects. Cotton fabrics are washable, which means you don't have to worry about food spills. The beautiful colors and patterns are a pleasure to work with, and we think you will enjoy coming up with different combinations to use in your table settings. Consider the dinnerware color and style when you make your choices. If you are making table linens for a gift, consider the personality, style preferences, and dinnerware of the recipient. Remember that it is not necessary to match colors exactly. In any color scheme, subtle changes in tone will actually enhance the palette.

You can purchase cotton quilting fabric in quilting shops and fabric chain stores. Quilting cottons are 42″ to 44″ wide, and this is the fabric width we allowed for in our fabric yardage calculations. Decorator cottons, which are 56″ to 60″ wide, can also be used; you may have to adjust the yardage if you use decorator fabrics.

Before you begin cutting or sewing, prewash your fabric in the washing machine using cold water and a small amount of detergent. Machine dry on the permanent press setting, remove promptly, and press well. Prewashing helps to remove any excess dye and will prevent the colors from bleeding later on.

This precaution is especially important in projects sewn from a combination of dark and light fabrics. Prewashing also shrinks and sets the threads. This makes reversible projects, such as placemats, more stable. You wouldn't want one side of the project to shrink at a different percentage than the other side when laundered.

## What About Stains?

Spills are bound to occur when you are dining. To avoid permanent stains on your table linens and napkins, consult the stain removal guide in your washing machine owner's manual or download a guide from the Internet. Look for stain removal products in the laundry aisle at the supermarket that you can apply immediately and then wait for up to a week before washing. Another option is to apply a surface protectant, such as Scotchgard spray, to newly sewn linens before the first use.

# basic how-tos

The tools, sewing methods, and construction techniques described here can be used for all the table topper projects in this book.

Read this chapter to become familiar with the techniques. Refer back to this chapter as needed when you are making specific projects.

# Cutting

Rotary cutting tools are a boon for measuring and cutting pieces of fabric accurately and quickly. You will need a rotary cutter with a new blade, a self-healing cutting mat, and rotary cutting rulers in several sizes. We suggest a 6″ × 24″ ruler for measuring and cutting strips of fabric. A 15″ square ruler is useful when making placemats, table mats, and runners. If you have never used a rotary cutter before, ask for a demonstration at the shop where you make your purchase. If you don't have rotary cutting tools, you can use a yardstick and a fabric marking pencil to measure and mark the fabric. Cut on the marked lines with sharp scissors. The project cutting guides describe which fabrics to use and what sizes to cut the pieces.

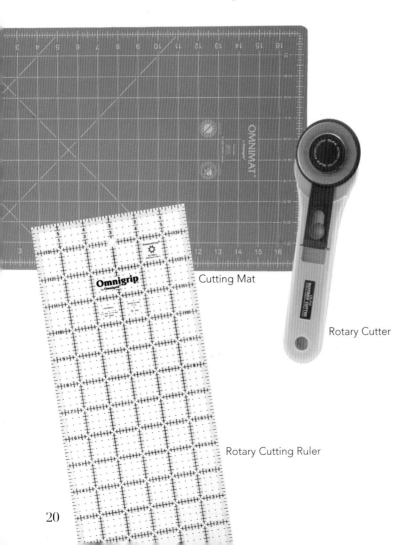

Cutting Mat

Rotary Cutter

Rotary Cutting Ruler

# Piecing and Pressing

To sew two pieces of fabric together, place the pieces right sides together, aligning the edges that are to be joined. Machine stitch ¼″ from the edge. Backtack at the beginning and end of the stitching line to secure the stitches, if desired. Using a dry iron, press the seam allowance toward the darker fabric. Press the seam again on the right side. If a project calls for multiple seams, be sure to press each seam as you go. Steam-press the entire project when it is complete.

# Seamed Edges

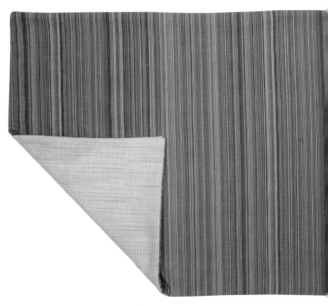

The seamed edge construction can be used for placemats, runners, table mats, napkins, and even small tablecloths. In a simple construction, two pieces of fabric—a front panel and a back panel—are cut to the same size and joined together. The fabrics can match or contrast. In more complex designs, the front panel is pieced from several different fabrics. For a professional finish, trim a pieced panel and a back panel to exactly the same size before you join them together.

1. Layer the front and back panels right sides together.

2. Begin stitching near the middle of a long edge, using a ¼″ seam allowance. Stitch all around the piece, pivoting at the corners (see How to Pivot, right), until the stitching line is 4″ from the starting point. Backtack and break off the threads.

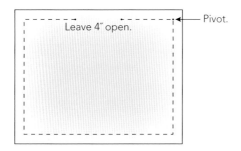

3. Trim the excess fabric from the corners. Press the seam allowances open as close to the corner as the tip of the iron will go.

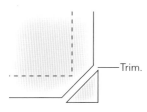

4. Turn the piece right side out through the opening. Use a point turner, or a ballpoint pen with the point retracted, to poke out the corners. Fold in the seam allowances at the opening and press well. Use a hand sewing needle and matching thread to slip-stitch the opening closed.

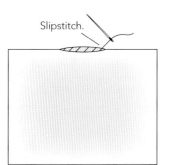

## How to Pivot

A pivot is a sewing maneuver that will help you create sharp corners on square and rectangular pillows. To gain control, slow down the sewing machine speed as you approach the corner. Stop sewing ¼″ from the fabric edge with the needle in the down position. Lift the presser foot and rotate the fabric one-quarter turn. Lower the presser foot and continue sewing along the adjacent edge.

Pivot ¼″ from the corner

Leave the needle down to pivot.

Resume stitching

Pivot the fabric, lower the foot, and resume sewing.

Seamed edge construction. Leave an opening along one long edge for turning.

# Bound Edges

A bound edge can be used on any table topper, but it typically appears on pieces that are interlined or lightly padded. In this construction method, borrowed from quiltmaking, the fabric and padding layers are sandwiched together and a narrow folded strip of fabric, or binding, encloses the raw edges. We use a single-fold binding (1½" cut width) when less bulk around the edges is desired.

## Binding Preparation

Layer the front and back panels wrong sides together, so that the batting or interlining (if used) is sandwiched in between. Use a rotary cutter and ruler to trim the edges and true up the corners, as necessary. Pin the layers together. The raw edges are now ready to be bound.

### wrapped-corner binding

1. Place a 1½"-wide binding strip on the front of the layered piece, right sides together and raw edges aligned. Allow the strip to extend ½" beyond the edge of the piece at each end.

2. Stitch ¼" from the edges through all the layers.

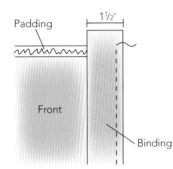

3. Press the remaining long edge of the binding ¼" to the wrong side.

4. Fold the binding onto the back of the layered piece. Line up the pressed fold on the stitching line and pin every few inches. Slipstitch the binding to the back of the piece with a hand sewing needle and matching thread.

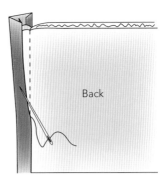

Back

5. Repeat Steps 1–4 to bind the opposite edge of the layered piece. Trim the ends of both bindings even with the edges of the piece. Bind the remaining edges, folding in the excess at the corners. The bindings will overlap at the corners.

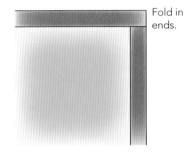

Fold in ends.

Wrapped Corner

### mock mitered-corner binding

1. Sew the binding strips into 1 continuous piece, using diagonal seams.

2. Press ¼" to the wrong side along 1 long edge of the strip.

3. Place the unfolded edge of the binding strip on the front of the layered piece, aligning the raw edges, as shown in Step 4 illustration. Begin stitching about 2" from the end of the binding strip, using a ¼" seam allowance.

4. As you come near the corner, slow down. Stop stitching exactly ¼″ from the corner edge. Backtack, cut the threads, and remove the piece from the machine.

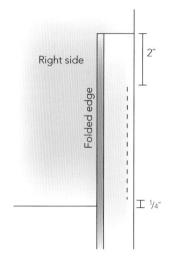

5. Rotate the piece so the sewn edge is on top and fold the binding strip up at a 45° angle.

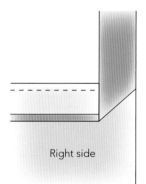

6. Fold the binding strip down to form a 90° angle at the corner. The edge of the binding strip must align with the side edge of the project. Pin if desired.

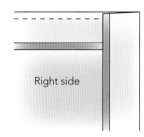

7. Machine stitch exactly ¼″ from the edge.

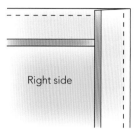

8. Repeat Steps 3–6 three times. When the stitching is 2″ from the starting point, fold in the starter end of the strip ¼″. Trim the other end of the strip, leaving a ½″ overlap. Stitch through all the layers.

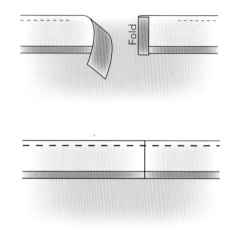

9. Fold the binding strip to the wrong side of the piece, enclosing the raw edges and forming a neat miter at each corner. Slipstitch the folded edge to the wrong side with a hand sewing needle and matching thread. Tuck in the excess fabric at the corners and secure with a few extra stitches.

Mock Mitered Corner

# Mitered Borders

Mitered corners add a handsome, professional look to the borders on all kinds of table toppers. Our technique uses four border strips. Each strip is cut several inches longer than the final finished edge of the table topper. The excess is trimmed off during the mitering process. The strip sizes in the project cutting guides include this extra allowance. Follow the instructions in On Your Own (below) to cut strips for custom sizes.

1. Mark the midpoint of 1 edge of the table topper with a pin. Mark the midpoint of the corresponding border strip with a pin.

2. Place the border strip on the table topper, wrong sides together, aligning the pins and the raw edges. Pin from the middle out to each edge, letting the excess border strip extend evenly at both ends.

3. Stitch along the pinned edge, using a $\frac{1}{4}''$ seam allowance and starting and stopping exactly $\frac{1}{4}''$ from each end. We recommend backtacking at the beginning and end of the seam to secure the stitches.

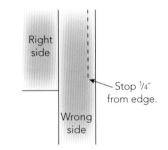

4. Press the seam allowance toward the border strip.

5. Repeat Steps 1–3 on an adjacent edge of the table topper. For this strip, the stitching should start exactly at the seamline of the first strip. Press the seam allowance toward the border strip.

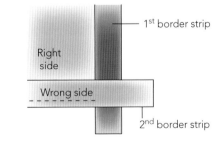

## On Your Own

Here's how to cut mitered border strips for a custom-size table topper. First, measure the length (L) and width (W) of the center piece of fabric. Decide on a border width and add $\frac{1}{2}''$ for seam allowances to determine the cut width of the border strips (B). Add L + B + B + 5″ * to determine the cut length of the 2 longer border strips. Add W + B + B + 5″ * to determine the cut length of the 2 shorter border strips. Cut 2 of each size strip. If the center piece of fabric is square, cut all 4 strips the same size.

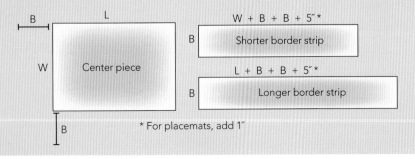

* For placemats, add 1″

6. Place the table topper right side up, so that 1 strip crosses over the other at a right angle. Fold the top border strip under itself, even with the strip underneath, to form a 45° angle.

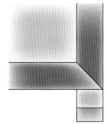

7. Use a right-angle triangle or grid ruler to check the angle and confirm that the corner is square. Adjust as needed. Press to set the crease.

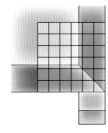

8. Fold the entire piece diagonally, right side in, bringing the long edges of the border strips together. Pin the border strips together along the pressed-in crease. Stitch along the crease line from the inside corner stitching line to the outside corner, backtacking at each end. Be careful not to stretch the fabric. Trim off the excess border strips ¼˝ beyond the stitching. Press the seam open.

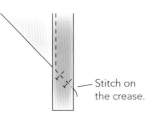

Stitch on the crease.

9. Repeat Steps 5–8 until all 4 corners are mitered and trimmed.

# Round Tablecloths

Round tablecloths are generally 60˝ to 70˝ in diameter for a dining table and up to 90˝ in diameter for a table covering that falls to the floor. The construction of a round tablecloth almost always involves one or two seams, but with careful planning, you can camouflage the seams in the drop. If possible, choose a fabric that is wider than the table diameter to start.

1. Measure the diameter of the tabletop (A) and the desired length of the drop (B).

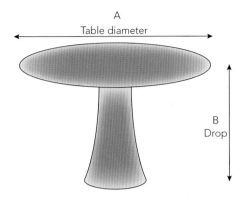

A
Table diameter

B
Drop

2. Add A + B + B to determine the diameter of the finished tablecloth. Add 1″ to the diameter to allow for a narrow hem.

3. Cut 2 pieces of fabric to this length. Trim off the selvages. Layer the pieces right sides together and stitch along 1 trimmed edge, using a ¼″ seam allowance. Press the seam allowance open.

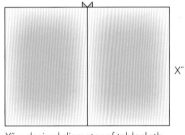

X″

X″ = desired diameter of tablecloth

4. Measure and cut a square from the large piece, so that the seam falls close to an outer edge.

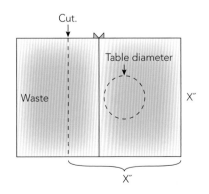

Cut.

Table diameter

Waste

X″

X″

To make squares for larger tables, you may need to cut 1 of the fabric pieces in half and join with 2 seams.

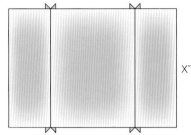

X″

X″ = desired diameter of tablecloth

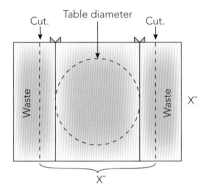

Cut.          Table diameter          Cut.

Waste     Waste

X″

X″

5. Fold the square into quarters.

Fold again into eighths. Measure from the folded point along the shorter edge. This length is one half the diameter of the tablecloth. Continue measuring from the folded point and marking this length with a pencil or chalk to mark an arc.

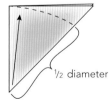

½ diameter

6. Cut along the marked line through several layers at a time until all the layers are cut.

7. Open out the cloth into a circle. Finish by sewing a clean finish hem (page 27).

# Clean Finish Hem

# Mitered-Corner Hem

The clean finish hem is often used on napkins that are sewn from a single layer of fabric. It is also an option for tablecloths, including round tablecloths.

- On a piece with straight edges, fold 1 edge a scant ¼″ to the wrong side. Fold in again ¼″ and stitch close to the folded edge. Pin or press the fabric before stitching if doing so helps you. Hem the opposite edge next. Hem the remaining edges, folding neatly at the corners.

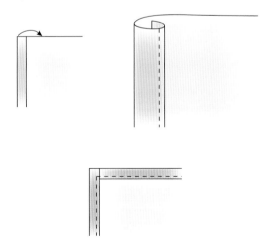

- On a rounded edge, machine baste through a single layer of fabric ¼″ from the edge all around. The long basting stitches will draw up the edge slightly and make it easier to handle. Fold the fabric to the wrong side on the stitched line and press with a dry iron. Fold in another ¼″ and stitch close to the edge all around.

Use a mitered-corner hem on square or rectangular pieces that are sewn from a single layer of fabric. The finished hem is 1″ deep, and the mitered seam, which appears on the underside, reduces excess bulk at the corners. We especially like napkins edged this way, but it is equally handsome for tablecloths, runners, and simple table mats. You'll need a piece of fabric that is 2½″ larger than the desired finished size to start.

1. Press each edge of the fabric ¼″ to the wrong side. Fold in 1″ to the wrong side and press again to set the crease.

2. Open out each 1″ fold. Align the 45° mark on a grid ruler with an edge of the fabric. Draw a pencil line through the intersection of the fold lines at 1 corner. Repeat at each corner.

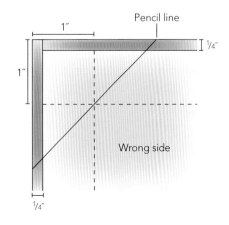

3. Fold 1 corner onto itself, right sides together. Stitch on the marked line through both layers, backtacking at the beginning and end of the stitching line.

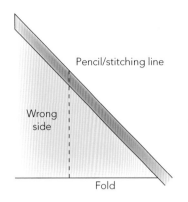

Pencil/stitching line

Wrong side

Fold

4. Trim ¼″ outside the stitching line.

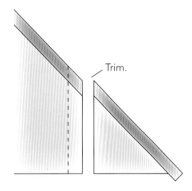

Trim.

5. Turn the corner right side out. Open and flatten the seam allowance. Press well. Repeat Steps 3–5 at each remaining corner. Topstitch ⅛″ from the inside edge of the hem all around.

⅛″

Reverse Side

# Napkin Ring Motifs

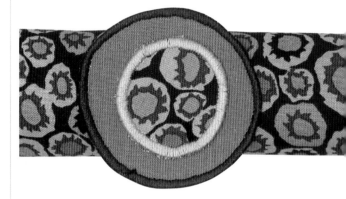

Our lightly padded napkin ring designs use fast2fuse, a new double-sided fusible stiff interfacing from C&T Publishing (see Sources, page 62). With fast2fuse, the fabric and interfacing layers fuse together quickly, ready for machine appliqué. The motifs are limited only by your imagination.

1. Trace the A piece pattern or design onto a piece of fast2fuse interfacing. Cut out on the pattern outline.

2. Cut out 2 pieces of fabric for the front and back of the napkin ring. Make each piece about ½″ larger than the fast2fuse cutout.

3. Protect your ironing board with a nonstick pressing sheet. Place the fast2fuse cutout on the pressing sheet. Layer 1 fabric piece on top of the cutout, right side up. Press with a hot, dry iron for 5 seconds. Allow the piece to cool.

4. Trim the fabric even with the edge of the cutout.

5. Place the cutout on the pressing sheet, fabric side down. Layer the remaining fabric piece on top, right side up. Press for 5 seconds to fuse. Allow to cool. Trim off the excess fabric.

6. Reset the iron to the steam setting. Press the cutout for 10 seconds on each side.

7. Install a zigzag foot on your sewing machine Set the machine to a wide zigzag stitch and a very short stitch length. Check your machine manual for the preferred settings. This wide, closely spaced zigzag stitch is called a machine satin stitch.

8. Using matching or contrasting thread, stitch around the edges of the motif. Add interior stitching lines to define the motif, as indicated on the pattern. Plan your stitching paths to define overlapping shapes.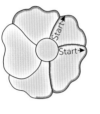

9. Steam press for 10 seconds on each side.

## Padding

Placemats, runners, and table mats are often interlined with batting or interfacing. Thin batting between two layers of fabric provides added heft and stability. You can purchase thin quilt batting by the yard or in packages at most sewing and quilting stores. Batting with fusible material on both sides must be pressed with a nonstick sheet when applied to the front of the project, and then can be fused to the back by ironing the finished piece. For stability without the bulk of padding, use a medium- or craft-weight fusible interfacing instead.

Follow the project instructions to cut the batting or interfacing to the correct size. Cut or piece the front of the placemat, runner, or table mat according to the project instructions. Place the front facedown on a flat ironing surface. Layer the batting or interfacing on top, fusible side down, and top with a pressing cloth, if desired, or with a nonstick sheet if a fusible side is exposed. Fuse the layers together following the manufacturer's instructions. Assemble the project as directed in the project instructions.

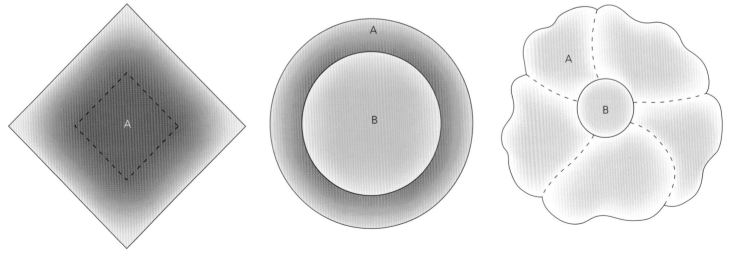

# table topper ·
# recipes

# easy placemat

Use this simple, easygoing style to showcase a special fabric, such as the decorator Asian print shown here. Choose different fabrics for the front and back to make a set of reversible placemats.

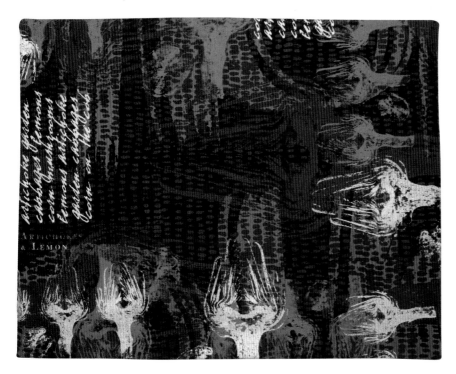

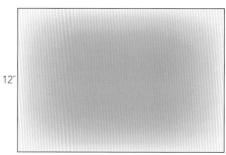

12″

18″

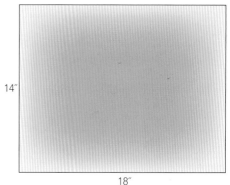

14″

18″

**PADDING:** Follow the Padding instructions on page 29, if desired.

**ASSEMBLY:** Follow the Seamed Edges instructions on page 20.

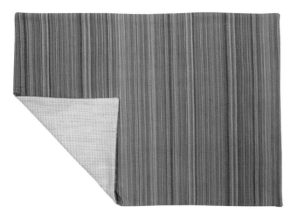

Reversible Placemat

## Materials

| FOR 2 PLACEMATS | MAIN FABRIC | BACKING FABRIC | THIN BATTING* |
|---|---|---|---|
| 18″ × 12″ | ½ yard | ½ yard | ½ yard |
| 18″ × 14″ | ½ yard | ½ yard | ½ yard |

*optional

## Cutting Guide

| FOR 2 PLACEMATS | MAIN FABRIC (cut 2) | BACKING FABRIC (cut 2) | THIN BATTING* (cut 2) |
|---|---|---|---|
| 18″ × 12″ | 18½″ × 12½″ | 18½″ × 12½″ | 18½″ × 12½″ |
| 18″ × 14″ | 18½″ × 14½″ | 18½″ × 14½″ | 18½″ × 14½″ |

*optional

# bound-edge placemat

For exuberant design energy, try a large print, such as this rustic cabbage rose fabric, on the relatively small canvas of a placemat. A contrasting binding around the edges helps contain these garden ramblers.

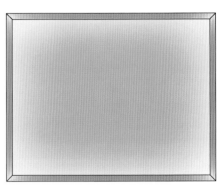

**PADDING:** Follow the Padding instructions on page 29, if desired.

**ASSEMBLY:** Follow the Bound Edges instructions on page 21.

## Materials

| FOR 2 PLACEMATS | MAIN FABRIC | BACKING FABRIC | BINDING FABRIC | THIN BATTING* |
|---|---|---|---|---|
| 18″ × 12″ | ½ yard | ½ yard | ¼ yard | ½ yard |
| 18″ × 14″ | ½ yard | ½ yard | ¼ yard | ½ yard |

*optional

## Cutting Guide

| FOR 2 PLACEMATS | MAIN FABRIC (cut 2) | BACKING FABRIC (cut 2) | BINDING STRIPS (cut 4) | THIN BATTING* (cut 2) |
|---|---|---|---|---|
| 18″ × 12″ | 18½″ × 12½″ | 18½″ × 12½″ | 1½″ × 42″ | 18½″ × 12½″ |
| 18″ × 14″ | 18½″ × 14½″ | 18½″ × 14½″ | 1½″ × 42″ | 18½″ × 14½″ |

*optional

# mitered-border placemat

The mitered-border construction is a classic look that works well with any combination of fabrics. Here, a "reads like a solid" red fabric frames a dramatic Asian floral print. Black in a placemat adds a sophisticated touch to evening dining.

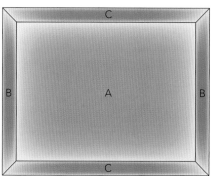

**FRONT:** Follow the Mitered Borders instructions on page 24.

**PADDING:** Follow the Padding instructions on page 29, if desired.

**ASSEMBLY:** Follow the Seamed Edges instructions on page 20.

## Materials

| FOR 2 PLACEMATS | MAIN FABRIC | BORDER FABRIC | BACKING FABRIC | THIN BATTING* |
|---|---|---|---|---|
| 18″ × 12″ | ⅜ yard | ⅜ yard | ½ yard | ½ yard |
| 18″ × 14″ | ⅜ yard | ⅜ yard | ½ yard | ½ yard |

*optional

## Cutting Guide

| FOR 2 PLACEMATS | MAIN FABRIC PANEL A (cut 2) | BORDER FABRIC | | BACKING FABRIC (cut 2) | THIN BATTING* (cut 2) |
|---|---|---|---|---|---|
| | | BORDER B (cut 4) | BORDER C (cut 4) | | |
| 18″ × 12″ | 15½″ × 9½″ | 2″ × 14½″** | 2″ × 20½″** | 18½″ × 12½″ | 18½″ × 12½″ |
| 18″ × 14″ | 15½″ × 11½″ | 2″ × 16½″** | 2″ × 20½″** | 18½″ × 14½″ | 18½″ × 14½″ |

*optional **includes mitering allowance

# inset-trim placemat

Narrow folded strips of fabric slipped into the border seams add an accent color to this placemat. We cut a striped fabric on the crosswise grain to produce a pulsating pattern around the edges.

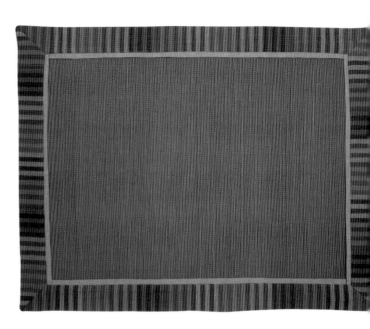

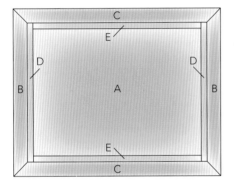

**INSET STRIPS:** Fold inset strips D and E in half lengthwise, wrong sides in, and press to set the crease. Place an E strip on each long edge of panel A, aligning the raw edges. Machine baste ¼″ from the edge through all layers. Baste the D strips to the short edges of panel A in the same way. Allow the strips to overlap at the corners.

**FRONT:** Follow the Mitered Borders instructions on page 24. The inset strips will become trapped in the seams.

**PADDING:** Follow the Padding instructions on page 29, if desired.

**ASSEMBLY:** Follow the Seamed Edges instructions on page 20.

## Materials

| FOR 2 PLACEMATS | MAIN FABRIC | BORDER FABRIC | INSET FABRIC | BACKING FABRIC | THIN BATTING* |
|---|---|---|---|---|---|
| 18″ × 12″ | ⅜ yard | ⅜ yard | ⅛ yard | ½ yard | ½ yard |
| 18″ × 14″ | ⅜ yard | ⅜ yard | ⅛ yard | ½ yard | ½ yard |

*optional

## Cutting Guide

| FOR 2 PLACEMATS | MAIN FABRIC | BORDER FABRIC | | INSET FABRIC | | BACKING FABRIC (cut 2) | THIN BATTING* (cut 2) |
| | PANEL A (cut 2) | BORDER B (cut 4) | BORDER C (cut 4) | INSET D (cut 4) | INSET E (cut 4) | | |
|---|---|---|---|---|---|---|---|
| 18″ × 12″ | 15½″ × 9½″ | 2″ × 14½″** | 2″ × 20½″** | 1″ × 9½″ | 1″ × 15½″ | 18½″ × 12½″ | 18½″ × 12½″ |
| 18″ × 14″ | 15½″ × 11½″ | 2″ × 16½″** | 2″ × 20½″** | 1″ × 11½″ | 1″ × 15½″ | 18½″ × 14½″ | 18½″ × 14½″ |

*optional **includes mitering allowance

# side-panels placemat

We like to think of side panels as bookends. They bracket the all-important theme fabric in a placemat. If you choose a busy, lively theme print, such as this 1950s kitchen design, try small dots, stripes, or a tone-on-tone print for the side panels.

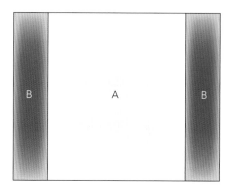

**FRONT:** Refer to Piecing and Pressing on page 20. Sew a panel B to each side edge of panel A. Press the seam allowances toward the darker fabric.

**PADDING:** Follow the Padding instructions on page 29, if desired.

**ASSEMBLY:** Follow the Seamed Edges instructions on page 20.

## Materials

| FOR 2 PLACEMATS | MAIN FABRIC | SIDE-PANEL FABRIC | BACKING FABRIC | THIN BATTING* |
|---|---|---|---|---|
| 18″ × 12″ | ⅜ yard | ¼ yard | ½ yard | ½ yard |
| 18″ × 14″ | ⅜ yard | ¼ yard | ½ yard | ½ yard |

*optional

## Cutting Guide

| FOR 2 PLACEMATS | MAIN FABRIC PANEL A (cut 2) | SIDE-PANEL FABRIC PANEL B (cut 4) | BACKING FABRIC (cut 2) | THIN BATTING* (cut 2) |
|---|---|---|---|---|
| 18″ × 12″ | 12½″ × 12½″ | 3½″ × 12 ½″ | 18½″ × 12½″ | 18½″ × 12½″ |
| 18″ × 14″ | 14½″ × 12½″ | 3½″ × 14 ½″ | 18½″ × 14½″ | 18½″ × 14½″ |

*optional

# log cabin placemat

In a traditional Log Cabin quilt block, the design builds out from a square patch at the center. We elongated the square into a rectangle to adapt the block construction to placemat dimensions. The varied "log" widths create movement and design interest.

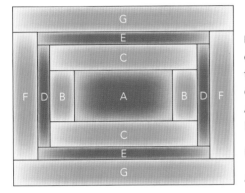

**FRONT:** Refer to Piecing and Pressing on page 20. Sew a B strip to each side edge of an A strip. Press the seam allowances toward the B strips. Sew C strips to the top and bottom edges of AB. Press toward C. Sew D strips to the side edges of ABC. Press toward D. Sew E strips to the top and bottom edges of ABCD. Press toward E. Sew F strips to the side edges of ABCDE. Press toward F. Sew G strips to the top and bottom edges of ABCDEF. Press toward G.

**PADDING:** Follow the Padding instructions on page 29, if desired.

**ASSEMBLY:** Follow the Seamed Edges instructions on page 20.

## Materials

| FOR 2 PLACEMATS | DARK FABRIC | MEDIUM FABRIC | BACKING FABRIC | THIN BATTING* |
|---|---|---|---|---|
| 18″ × 12″ | ¼ yard | ⅓ yard | ½ yard | ½ yard |
| 18″ × 14″ | ¼ yard | ½ yard | ½ yard | ½ yard |

*optional

## Cutting Guide

| FOR 2 PLACEMATS | DARK FABRIC | | MEDIUM FABRIC | BACKING FABRIC (cut 2) | THIN BATTING* (cut 2) |
|---|---|---|---|---|---|
| | CENTER (cut 2) | STRIPS (cut 4 of each) | STRIPS (cut 4 of each) | | |
| 18″ × 12″ | A 8½″ × 2½″ | D 1½″ × 6½″ | B 2½″ × 2½″ | 18½″ × 12½″ | 18½″ × 12½″ |
| | | E 1½″ × 14½″ | C 2½″ × 12½″ | | |
| | | | F 2½″ × 8½″ | | |
| | | | G 2½″ × 18½″ | | |
| 18″ × 14″ | A 8½″ × 4½″ | D 1½″ × 8½″ | B 2½″ × 4½″ | 18½″ × 14½″ | 18½″ × 14½″ |
| | | E 1½″ × 14½″ | C 2½″ × 12½″ | | |
| | | | F 2½″ × 10½″ | | |
| | | | G 2½″ × 18½″ | | |

*optional

# provence stripes placemat

Fabric strips of different widths are pieced together to create this informal placemat pattern. A Provence-inspired wallpaper print actually gave us two fabrics in one—a tiny floral repeat and the larger sunflower print. The remaining fabric colors coordinate with it.

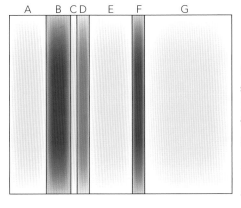

FRONT: Refer to Piecing and Pressing on page 20. Arrange strips A through G side by side, as shown in the diagram. Make sure the printed patterns are facing in the direction desired. Sew A to B. Press the seam allowance toward the darker fabric. Sew a C strip to AB. Press toward the darker fabric. Continue adding the pieces in order, pressing after each addition.

PADDING: Follow the Padding instructions on page 29, if desired.

ASSEMBLY: Follow the Seamed Edges instructions on page 20.

## Materials

| FOR 2 PLACEMATS | MAIN FABRIC | 3 ACCENT FABRICS | BACKING FABRIC | THIN BATTING* |
|---|---|---|---|---|
| 18″ × 12″ | ⅝ yard | ¼ yard each | ½ yard | ½ yard |
| 18″ × 14″ | ⅝ yard | ¼ yard each | ½ yard | ½ yard |

*optional

## Cutting Guide

| FOR 2 PLACEMATS | MAIN FABRIC STRIPS (cut 2 of each) | 3 ACCENT FABRICS STRIPS (cut 2 of each) | BACKING FABRIC (cut 2) | THIN BATTING* (cut 2) |
|---|---|---|---|---|
| 18″ × 12″ | A 3½″ × 12½″ | B 2½″ × 12½″ | 18½″ × 12½″ | 18½″ × 12½″ |
| | E 4″ × 12½″ | F 1½″ × 12½″ | | |
| | G 7½″ × 12½″ | C 1″ × 12½″ | | |
| | | D 1½″ × 12½″ | | |
| 18″ × 14″ | A 3½″ × 14½″ | B 2½″ × 14½″ | 18½″ × 14½″ | 18½″ × 14½″ |
| | E 4″ × 14½″ | F 1½″ × 14½″ | | |
| | G 7½″ × 14½″ | C 1″ × 14½″ | | |
| | | D 1½″ × 14½″ | | |

*optional

# solid-stripes placemat

This version of our informal striped placemat uses solid fabrics. A mix of dark, medium, and light tones in one color family is the key to creating a pleasing harmony.

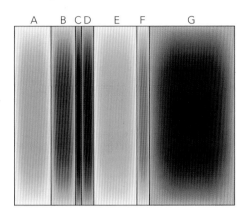

**FRONT:** Refer to Piecing and Pressing on page 20. Arrange strips A through G side by side, as shown in the diagram. Sew A to B. Press the seam allowance toward the darker fabric. Sew a C strip to AB. Press toward the darker fabric. Continue adding the pieces in order, pressing after each addition.

## Materials

| FOR 2 PLACEMATS | MAIN FABRIC | 4 ACCENT FABRICS | BACKING FABRIC | THIN BATTING* |
|---|---|---|---|---|
| 18″ × 12″ | ⅓ yard | ⅛ to ¼ yard each | ½ yard | ½ yard |
| 18″ × 14″ | ⅓ yard | ⅛ to ¼ yard each | ½ yard | ½ yard |

*optional

**PADDING:** Follow the Padding instructions on page 29, if desired.

**ASSEMBLY:** Follow the Seamed Edges instructions on page 20.

## Cutting Guide

| FOR 2 PLACEMATS | MAIN FABRIC STRIPS (cut 2 of each) | 4 ACCENT FABRICS STRIPS (cut 2 of each) | BACKING FABRIC (cut 2) | THIN BATTING* (cut 2) |
|---|---|---|---|---|
| 18″ × 12″ | C 1″ × 12½″ | A 3½″ × 12½″ | 18½″ × 12½″ | 18½″ × 12½″ |
|  | G 7½″ × 12½″ | B 2½″ × 12½″ |  |  |
|  |  | F 1½″ × 12½″ |  |  |
|  |  | D 1½″ × 12½″ |  |  |
|  |  | E 4″ × 12½″ |  |  |
| 18″ × 14″ | C 1″ × 14½″ | A 3½″ × 14½″ | 18½″ × 14½″ | 18½″ × 14½″ |
|  | G 7½″ × 14½″ | B 2½″ × 14½″ |  |  |
|  |  | F 1½″ × 14½ |  |  |
|  |  | D 1½″ × 14½″ |  |  |
|  |  | E 4″ × 14½″ |  |  |

*optional

# rectangular tablecloth

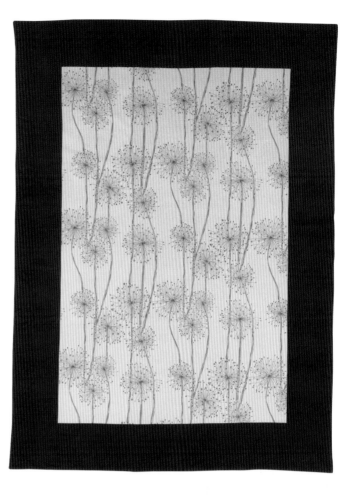

We custom-sized this tablecloth to fit Valori's 40″ × 58″ dining table. The center panel fits the top of the table perfectly, and the dark border overhangs the edge. You can easily adapt the cutting guide for any rectangular dining table up to 40″ wide.

## Materials

| FOR 1 TABLE CLOTH | MAIN FABRIC | BORDER FABRIC | BACKING FABRIC* |
|---|---|---|---|
| 56″ × 74″ (custom size; fits a 40″ × 58″ table) | 1¾ yards | 1¾ yards | 3¼ yards |

*optional

## Cutting Guide

| FOR 1 TABLE CLOTH | MAIN FABRIC CENTER PANEL (cut 1) | BORDER FABRIC STRIPS (cut 7) | SIDE BORDERS (make 2) | TOP AND BOTTOM BORDERS (cut 2) | BACKING FABRIC* (cut 2) |
|---|---|---|---|---|---|
| 56″ × 74″ (custom size; fits a 40″ × 58″ table) | 40½″ × 58½″ | 8½″ × width of fabric — Join strips end to end to make 1 long strip. Cut to specified border lengths. | 8½″ × 80½″ | 8½″ × 62½″ | 56½″ × 37½″ — Join pieces to make 1 piece 56½″ × 74½″ |

*optional

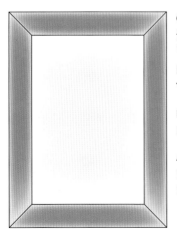

CUSTOM SIZING: Measure the tabletop length and add ½″ for seam allowances (L). Measure the tabletop width and add ½″ for seam allowances (W). Allow extra fabric if your table is larger than the sample table. Follow the instructions in On Your Own (page 24) to cut the border strips.

FRONT: Refer to Piecing and Pressing on page 20. Follow the Mitered Borders instructions on page 24.

ASSEMBLY: Follow the Seamed Edges instructions on page 20 if using a backing. Otherwise, follow the Clean Finish Hem instructions on page 27.

# square tablecloth

Make this casual tablecloth for luncheons or picnics. The deep mitered border extends the size of the center square, which is cut from a single piece of 42"-wide fabric. We choose green striped fabric to coordinate with the vegetable print.

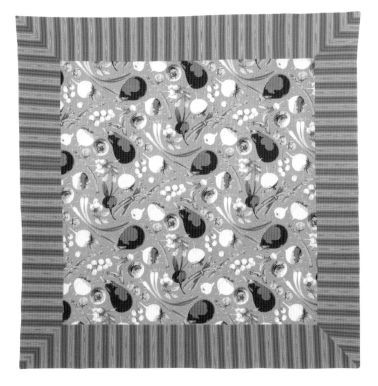

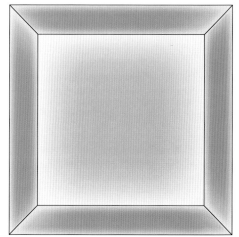

FRONT: Follow the Mitered Borders instructions on page 24.

ASSEMBLY: Follow the Seamed Edges instructions on page 20 if using a backing. Otherwise, follow the Clean Finish Hem instructions on page 27.

## Materials

| FOR 1 TABLE CLOTH | MAIN FABRIC | BORDER FABRIC | BACKING FABRIC* 60" wide** |
|---|---|---|---|
| 55" × 55" | 1¼ yards | 1⅜ yards | 1⅝ yards |

*optional     ** Design requires minimum of 55½" cut width.

## Cutting Guide

| FOR 1 TABLE CLOTH | MAIN FABRIC CENTER PANEL (cut 1) | BORDER FABRIC STRIPS (cut 4) | BORDERS (make 4) | BACKING FABRIC* (cut 1) |
|---|---|---|---|---|
| 55" × 55" (custom size) | 41½" × 41½" | 7½" × width of fabric | 7½" × 61½" | 55½" × 55½" |
| | | Join strips end to end to make 1 long strip. Cut to specified border lengths. | | |

*optional

# runner-inset tablecloth

This tablecloth style allows you to expand the theme of the table. We chose a dark, quiet print for the runner inset to showcase flowers and candles. The printed fabric works well under solid-color plates. You can make napkins from the leftover inset fabric to complete the ensemble.

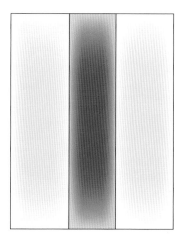

FRONT: Refer to Piecing and Pressing on page 20. Sew a side panel to each long edge of the inset panel. Press.

ASSEMBLY: Follow the Seamed Edges instructions on page 20 if using a backing. Otherwise, follow the Clean Finish Hem instructions on page 27.

## Materials

| FOR 1 TABLECLOTH | MAIN FABRIC | INSET FABRIC | BACKING FABRIC* |
|---|---|---|---|
| 56″ × 74″ (custom size) | 2¼ yards | 2¼ yards | 3¼ yards |
| 70″ × 90″ | 5¼ yards | 2⅝ yards | 5¼ yards |
| 70″ × 126″ | 7¼ yards | 3⅝ yards | 7¼ yards |

*optional

## Cutting Guide

| FOR 1 TABLECLOTH | MAIN FABRIC SIDE PANELS (cut 2) | INSET FABRIC INSET PANEL (cut 1) | BACKING FABRIC* (cut 2) |
|---|---|---|---|
| 56″ × 74″ (custom size) | 20½″ × 74½″ | 16½″ × 74½″ | 56½″ × 37½″ Join pieces to make 1 piece 56½″ × 74½″. |
| 70″ × 90″ | 26½″ × 90½″ | 18½″ × 90½″ | 35½″ × 90½″ Join pieces to make 1 piece 70½″ × 90½″. |
| 70″ × 126″ | 26½″ × 126½″ | 18½″ × 126½″ | 35½″ × 126½″ Join pieces to make 1 piece 70½″ × 126½″. |

*optional

# reversible table topper

A reversible table topper takes no longer to sew, yet you get two looks in one. Choose compatible fabrics to avoid unsightly color clashes at the seamline. Use this two-for-one technique with any of our tablecloth or table topper designs to build your collection. Tassels at the corners add a dressy touch.

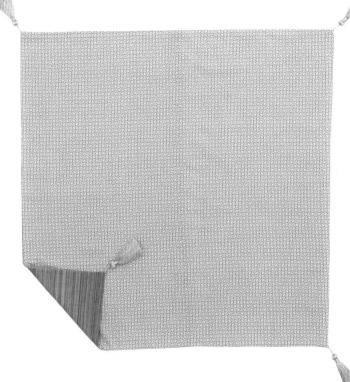

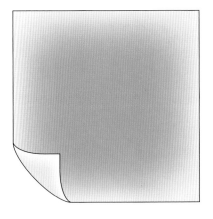

ASSEMBLY: Follow the Seamed Edges instructions on page 20. Tassels can be basted in place at the corners before the edges are sewn together, or you can attach the tassels to buttons at the corners after assembly, for ease in removal for washing.

## Materials

| FOR 1 TABLE TOPPER | FRONT FABRIC | REVERSE-SIDE FABRIC |
| --- | --- | --- |
| 24″ × 24″ | ¾ yard | ¾ yard |
| 36″ × 36″ | 1⅛ yards | 1⅛ yards |
| 42″ × 42″ | 1¼ yards | 1¼ yards |

*optional: 4 tassels

## Cutting Guide

| FOR 1 TABLE TOPPER | FRONT FABRIC (cut 1) | REVERSE-SIDE FABRIC (cut 1) |
| --- | --- | --- |
| 24″ × 24″ | 24½″ × 24½″ | 24½″ × 24½″ |
| 36″ × 36″ | 36½″ × 36½″ | 36½″ × 36½″ |
| 42″ × 42″ | 42½″ × 42½″ | 42½″ × 42½″ |

# round tablecloth

Round tablecloths can drop 6″ to 8″ below the table rim or reach to the floor. We give instructions for several sizes below. To make a custom size for a particular table, follow the Round Tablecloths instructions on page 25. The ensemble shown here features a 70″ round tablecloth and a 40″ × 40″ square topper set on point. The tabletop is 22″ round, and the drop to the floor is 24″.

## Materials

| FOR 1 TABLECLOTH | MAIN FABRIC | BACKING FABRIC* |
|---|---|---|
| 36″ ROUND | 1¼ yards | 1¼ yards |
| 48″ ROUND | 2⅞ yards | 2⅞ yards |
| 70″ ROUND | 4⅛ yards | 4⅛ yards |

*optional

## Cutting Guide

| FOR 1 TABLECLOTH | MAIN FABRIC (cut 1 of each) | BACKING FABRIC* |
|---|---|---|
| 36″ ROUND | 38″ × 38″ | 38″ × 38″ |
| 48″ ROUND | 42″ × 50″ | 42″ × 50″ |
| | 8½″ × 50″ | 8½″ × 50″ |
| | Join pieces together to make a 50″ × 50″ square. | Join pieces together to make a 50″ × 50″ square. |
| 70″ ROUND | 42″ × 72″ | 42″ × 72″ |
| | 30½″ × 72″ | 30½″ × 72″ |
| | Join pieces together to make a 72″ × 72″ square. | Join pieces together to make a 72″ × 72″ square. |

*optional

CIRCLE CUTTING: Follow the Round Tablecloths instructions on page 25. Cut a circle from the main fabric and the backing fabric, if using.

ASSEMBLY: Follow the Seamed Edges instructions on page 20 if using a backing. Otherwise, follow the Clean Finish Hem instructions on page 27.

# four seasons table runners

One table + four runners = four terrific seasonal looks. Pick four printed fabrics—one for each season—to create this rotating wardrobe for your dining table or buffet. You don't have to be too literal when choosing prints. Let the color, mood, and subject matter of the prints speak to you. You may want to expand this basic collection to include favorite holidays.

**FRONT:** Refer to Piecing and Pressing on page 20. Sew a B strip to the top and bottom edges of A. Press the seam allowances toward B. Sew C strips to each side edge of the AB unit. Press toward C. Sew D strips to the top and bottom edges of ABC. Press toward D. Sew E strips to the side edges of ABCD. Press toward E.

**PADDING:** Follow the Padding instructions on page 29, if desired.

**ASSEMBLY:** Follow the Seamed Edges instructions on page 20.

## Materials

| FOR 1 RUNNER | MAIN AND BACKING FABRIC | INNER BORDER FABRIC | OUTER BORDER FABRIC | THIN BATTING* |
|---|---|---|---|---|
| 14″ × 62″ | 1⅞ yards | ¼ yard | ⅓ yard | 1⅞ yards |

*optional

## Cutting Guide

| FOR 1 RUNNER | MAIN FABRIC | | INNER BORDER FABRIC | | OUTER BORDER FABRIC | | THIN BATTING* (cut 1) |
|---|---|---|---|---|---|---|---|
| | CENTER PANEL (cut 1) | BACKING | STRIPS (cut 4) | BORDER (make 2) | STRIPS (cut 4) | BORDER (make 2) | |
| 14″ × 62″ | 8½″ × 56½″ | 14½″ × 62½″ | 1½″ × 42″ | B 1½″ × 56½″ | 2½″ × 42″ | D 2½″ × 58½″ | 14½″ × 62½″ |
| | | | | C 1½″ × 10½″ | | E 2½″ × 14½″ | |
| | | | | Join strips end to end to make 1 long strip. Cut to border lengths as specified. | | Join strips end to end to make 1 long strip. Cut to border lengths as specified. | |

*optional

Spring

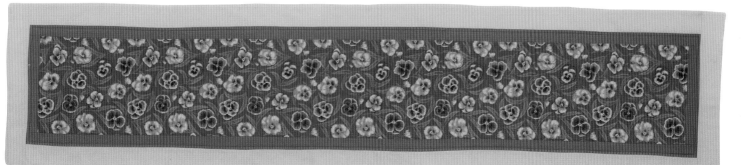

Summer

Fall

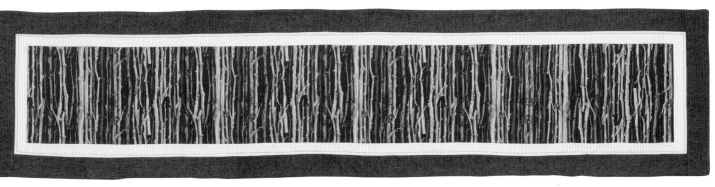

Winter

# twelve-block table runner

Explore a new color palette when you sew this easy patchwork design. Watery blues and greens transport us to the beach in an instant, even when we are time zones away. As you work with different colors, your own preferences will emerge. You will naturally choose colors that bring you refreshment.

Row 1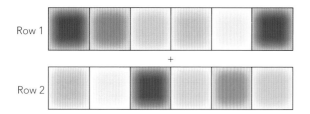

+

Row 2

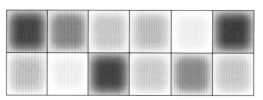

## Materials

| FOR 1 RUNNER | 6 ASSORTED FABRICS | BACKING FABRIC | THIN BATTING* |
|---|---|---|---|
| 16″ × 48″ | ⅓ yard each | ⅞ yard | 1⅜ yards |

*optional

## Cutting Guide

| FOR 1 RUNNER | 6 ASSORTED FABRICS PATCHWORK SQUARES (cut 2 of each fabric) | BACKING FABRIC (cut 2) | THIN BATTING* (cut 1) |
|---|---|---|---|
| 16″ × 48″ | 8½″ × 8½″ | 16½″ × 24½″ Join pieces to make 1 piece 16½″ × 48½″. | 16½″ × 48½″ |

*optional

FRONT: Refer to Piecing and Pressing on page 20. Arrange 12 assorted squares into 2 rows, as shown. Rearrange the squares as desired until the design is pleasing to you. Sew the squares in Row 1 end to end. Press the seam allowances in one direction. Sew the squares in Row 2 end to end. Press the seam allowances in the opposite direction. Join the rows together, butting the seams. Press.

ASSEMBLY: Follow the Seamed Edges instructions on page 20.

# four-patch table runner

Holiday reds and greens are one example of a color palette you might choose for this patchwork runner. Six different fabrics encourage you to experiment. The smaller patches are ideal for using up scraps.

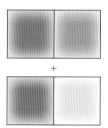

**FOUR-PATCH BLOCKS:** Refer to Piecing and Pressing on page 20. Arrange 4 different small squares in a four-patch as shown. Sew the squares together in pairs. Press the seam allowances in opposite directions. Sew the pairs together, butting the seams. Press. Make 4 four-patch blocks.

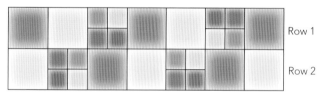

Row 1

Row 2

**FRONT:** Arrange 10 large squares and 4 four-patch blocks in 2 rows, as shown or as desired. Sew the squares in Row 1 end to end. Press the seam allowances in 1 direction. Sew the squares in Row 2 end to end. Press the seam allowances in the opposite direction. Join the rows together, butting the seams. Press.

**PADDING:** Follow the Padding instructions on page 29, if desired.

**ASSEMBLY:** Follow the Seamed Edges instructions on page 20.

## Materials

| FOR 1 RUNNER | FABRIC 1 | FABRIC 2 | 4 ASSORTED FABRICS | BACKING FABRIC | THIN BATTING* |
|---|---|---|---|---|---|
| 16″ × 56″ | ⅓ yard | ⅓ yard | ¼ yard each | 1 yard | 1⅝ yards |

*optional

## Cutting Guide

| FOR 1 RUNNER | FABRICS 1 AND 2 LARGE SQUARES (cut 5 of each fabric) | 4 ASSORTED FABRICS SMALL SQUARES (cut 4 of each fabric) | BACKING FABRIC (cut 2) | THIN BATTING* (cut 1) |
|---|---|---|---|---|
| 16″ × 56″ | 8½″ × 8½″ | 4½″ × 4½″ | 16½″ × 28½″ <br><br> Join pieces to make 1 piece 16½″ × 56½″. | 16½″ × 56½″ |

*optional

# striped table runner

A striped runner is a variation on our Provence Stripes placemat design (page 37). Start with a theme fabric with several colors in it. Select solids in the same colors to build a palette for strip piecing. The informal piecing sequence makes it easy to add or remove pieces to achieve the precise runner length you require.

## Materials

| FOR 1 RUNNER | THEME FABRIC | SOLID ACCENT FABRICS | | | | | BACKING FABRIC (44" wide)** | THIN BATTING* |
| | | 1 | 2 | 3 | 4 | 5 | | |
|---|---|---|---|---|---|---|---|---|
| 14" × 42" | ½ yard | ¼ yard | ¼ yard | ¼ yard | ¼ yard | ¼ yard | ½ yard | ½ yard |

*optional    ** Design requires minimum of 42½" cut width.

## Cutting Guide

| FOR 1 RUNNER | THEME FABRIC PANELS (cut 1 of each) | SOLID ACCENT FABRIC STRIPS (cut 1 of each) | | | | | BACKING FABRIC (cut 1) | THIN BATTING* (cut 1) |
| | | 1 | 2 | 3 | 4 | 5 | | |
|---|---|---|---|---|---|---|---|---|
| 14" × 42" | A<br>9½" × 14½" | B<br>1½" × 14½" | C<br>1½" × 14½" | D<br>3½" × 14½" | E<br>2" × 14½" | F<br>1½" × 14½" | 14½" × 42½" | 14½" × 42½" |
| | H<br>4½" × 14½" | G<br>1" × 14½" | I<br>1½" × 14½" | J<br>2½" × 14½" | K<br>5" × 14½" | L<br>1" × 14½" | | |
| | P<br>7½" × 14½" | M<br>2½" × 14½" | N<br>3½" × 14½" | O<br>1½" × 14½" | | | | |

*optional

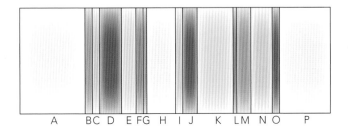

A   BC D E FG H I J K LM N O P

FRONT: Refer to Piecing and Pressing on page 20. Arrange pieces A through P side by side, as shown. Sew A to B. Press the seam allowance toward B. Sew C to the AB unit. Press the seam allowance toward C. Continue adding pieces, pressing in the same direction after each addition.

PADDING: Follow the Padding instructions on page 29, if desired.

ASSEMBLY: Follow the Seamed Edges instructions on page 20.

# cottage-style table runner

A runner sewn from warm-colored prints is especially beautiful on a natural wood table. The understated palette and pointed ends—easy to cut with a rotary grid ruler—add quiet sophistication. A contrasting binding gives the illusion of an outer border.

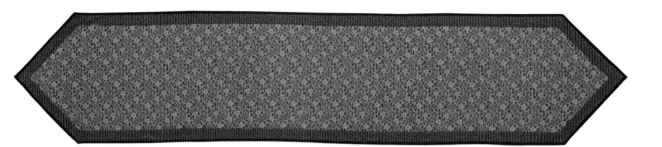

**SHAPE THE POINTS:** Place the center panel on a cutting mat. At one end, make light pencil marks on the 3 fabric edges 7½″ from the corners. Align the corner of a grid ruler on the marks and cut with a rotary cutter to create the point. Repeat at the other end of the panel.

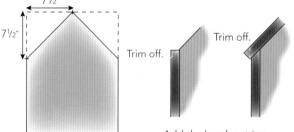

Shape the points.

Trim off.

Trim off.

Add the border strips.

**FRONT:** Refer to Piecing and Pressing on page 20. Sew each side border to 1 long edge of the center panel, allowing the excess border strip to extend evenly at each end. Press toward the border. Use a rotary cutter and ruler to trim off the excess side border even with the edge of the point. Sew a point border to each remaining edge, pressing and trimming after each addition as shown.

**PADDING:** Follow the Padding instructions on page 29, if desired. Use the front as a template to cut the batting.

**ASSEMBLY:** Use the front as a template to cut the backing. Follow the Wrapped-Corner Binding instructions on page 22. Bind the long edges first and then the points.

## Materials

| FOR 1 RUNNER | MAIN AND BACKING FABRIC | BORDER FABRIC | BINDING | THIN BATTING* |
|---|---|---|---|---|
| 15½″ × 72½″ | 2⅛ yards | ⅓ yard | ¼ yard | 2⅛ yards |

*optional

## Cutting Guide

| FOR 1 RUNNER | MAIN FABRIC | | BORDER FABRIC | | BINDING | | THIN BATTING* (cut 1) |
|---|---|---|---|---|---|---|---|
| | CENTER PANEL (cut 1) | BACKING FABRIC (cut 1) | STRIPS (cut 4) | BORDERS | STRIPS (cut 4) | BINDING | |
| 15½″ × 72½″ | 12½″ × 69½″ | 15½″ × 72½″ | 2″ × 42″ | Side borders, 2″ × 57″ (make 2) | 1½″ × 42″ | Side bindings, 1½″ × 57″ (make 2) | 15½″ × 72½″ |
| | | | | Point borders, 2″ × 12″ (make 4) | | Point bindings, 1½″ × 13″ (make 4) | |
| | | | | Join strips end to end to make 1 long strip. Cut to border lengths as specified. | | Join strips end to end to make 1 long strip. Cut to border lengths as specified. | |

*optional

# tuscan table runner

The patchwork at each end of this runner looks complicated but is easy to sew. To see the glazed pitcher and flowers that inspired this earthy palette, turn to page 13.

## Materials

| FOR 1 RUNNER | MAIN AND BACKING FABRIC | 4 ACCENT FABRICS | THIN BATTING* |
|---|---|---|---|
| 12″ × 51″ | 1⅓ yards | ⅛ yard each | 1⅝ yards |

*optional

## Cutting Guide

| FOR 1 RUNNER | MAIN FABRIC | | ACCENT FABRICS | | | | THIN BATTING* |
|---|---|---|---|---|---|---|---|
| | FRONT | BACKING | 1 | 2 | 3 | 4 | |
| 12″ × 51″ | A 12½″ × 42½″ (cut 1) | Cut 2 pieces 12½″ × 25¾″ | B 1″ × 10½″ (cut 4) | C 1″ × 10½″ (cut 4) | D 1″ × 10½″ (cut 4) | F 1″ × 1″ (cut 6) | 12½″ × 51″ |
| | E 2″ × 10½″ (cut 4) | Join pieces to make 1 piece 12½″ × 51½″. | | | | G 2″ × 2″ (cut 2) | |

*optional

**SHAPE THE POINTS:** Place the center panel on a cutting mat. At 1 end, make light pencil marks on the 3 fabric edges 6¼″ from the corners. Align the corner of a grid ruler on the marks and cut with a rotary cutter to create the point. Repeat at the other end of the panel.

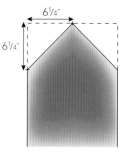

**UNITS:** Refer to Pressing and Piecing on page 20. Sew the accent squares to the strips and press the seam allowances toward the strips. Make 2 BF units, 2 CF units, 2 DF units, and 2 EG units.

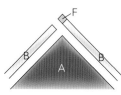

Join the units.

**FRONT:** Lay out panel A, the units, and the remaining B, C, D, and E strips as shown. Sew B to A along one edge of the point, letting the excess extend beyond the long side edge of A. Press toward A. Sew BF to the other edge of the point. Press toward A. Continue in this manner to add C and CF, D and DF, and E and EF, pressing after each addition. Piece the opposite point in the same way. Use the rotary cutter and ruler to trim off the excess even with the long side edges of A.

**PADDING:** Follow the Padding instructions on page 29. Use the pieced front as a template to cut the batting.

**ASSEMBLY:** Follow the Seamed Edges instructions on page 20. Use the pieced front as a template to cut the backing.

# table mat

Table mats turn everyday dining into a festive occasion.
Set the mood with the theme print of your choice,
such as the dramatic Asian floral print shown here.

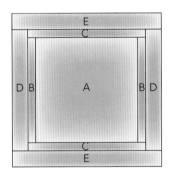

**FRONT:** Refer to Piecing and Pressing on page 20. Sew the B inner borders to the side edges of panel A. Press toward B. Sew the C inner borders to the top and bottom edges of panel A. Press toward C. Add the D and E outer borders in the same way, pressing after each addition.

**PADDING:** Follow the Padding instructions on page 29. Use the pieced front as a template to cut the batting.

**ASSEMBLY:** Follow the Seamed Edges instructions on page 20.

## Materials

| FOR 1 CENTERPIECE | MAIN AND BACKING FABRIC | INNER BORDER FABRIC | OUTER BORDER FABRIC | THIN BATTING* |
|---|---|---|---|---|
| 19″ × 19″ | ⅔ yard | ¼ yard | ¼ yard | ⅔ yard |

*optional

## Cutting Guide

| FOR 1 CENTERPIECE | MAIN FABRIC | | INNER BORDER STRIPS (cut 2 of each) | OUTER BORDER STRIPS (cut 2 of each) | THIN BATTING* (cut 1) |
|---|---|---|---|---|---|
| | PANEL A (cut 1) | BACKING (cut 1) | | | |
| 19″ × 19″ | 13½″ × 13½″ | 19½″ × 19½″ | B 1½″ × 13½″ | D 2½″ × 15½″ | 19½″ × 19½″ |
| | | | C 1½″ × 15½″ | E 2½″ × 19½″ | |

*optional

# hemmed napkins

Your table settings will never look dull when you have a selection of cloth napkins to choose from. Napkins with hemmed edges are so easy to sew. Make them this afternoon, use them tonight!

## Materials

| FOR 4 NAPKINS | FABRIC |
|---|---|
| 18″ × 18″ | 1¼ yards |
| 20″ × 20″ | 1⅓ yards |
| 22″ × 22″ | 2⅔ yards |

## Cutting Guide

| FOR 4 NAPKINS | FABRIC (cut 4) |
|---|---|
| 18″ × 18″ | 19″ × 19″ |
| 20″ × 20″ | 21″ × 21″ |
| 22″ × 22″ | 23″ × 23″ |

HEMMING: Follow the Clean Finish Hem instructions on page 27. Hem all 4 edges of each napkin square.

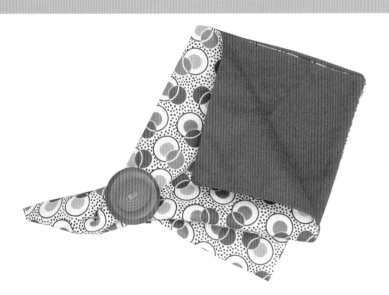

# reversible napkins

This easy-to-sew construction gives your table setting two napkin looks in one. Fold the napkin so that one fabric shows. Your guests will discover the other fabric as the meal unfolds. Prewash both fabrics to prevent shrinking and shifting after you sew.

ASSEMBLY: Follow the Seamed Edges instructions on page 20. For each napkin, sew a main fabric square to a contrast fabric square.

## Materials

| FOR 4 NAPKINS | MAIN FABRIC | CONTRAST FABRIC |
|---|---|---|
| 18″ × 18″ | 1¼ yards | 1¼ yards |
| 20″ × 20″ | 1¼ yards | 1¼ yards |
| 22″ × 22″ | 2⅝ yards | 2⅝ yards |

## Cutting Guide

| FOR 4 NAPKINS | MAIN FABRIC (cut 4) | CONTRAST FABRIC (cut 4) |
|---|---|---|
| 18″ × 18″ | 18½″ × 18½″ | 18½″ × 18½″ |
| 20″ × 20″ | 20½″ × 20½″ | 20½″ × 20½″ |
| 22″ × 22″ | 22½″ × 22½″ | 22½″ × 22½″ |

# mitered-corner napkins

## Materials

| FOR 4 NAPKINS | FABRIC |
|---|---|
| 18″ × 18″ | 1¼ yards |
| 20″ × 20″ | 2⅝ yards |
| 22″ × 22″ | 3 yards |

## Cutting Guide

| FOR 4 NAPKINS | FABRIC (cut 4) |
|---|---|
| 18″ × 18″ | 20½″ × 20½″ |
| 20″ × 20″ | 22½″ × 22½″ |
| 22″ × 22″ | 24½″ × 24½″ |

**ASSEMBLY:** Follow the Mitered-Corner Hem instructions on page 27.

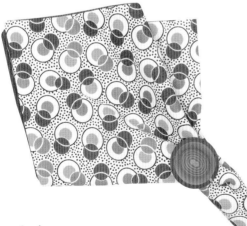

# button napkin rings

Shop for unusual decorative or vintage buttons at estate sales, in thrift shops, and online, or simply rummage through your own button box for hidden treasures. Each napkin ring requires one large shank-type button. To give your dining table a playful look, assemble a group of buttons that are compatible but not identical.

## Materials

| FOR 4 NAPKIN RINGS | GROSGRAIN RIBBON |
|---|---|
| 4 vintage or decorative shank-style buttons | 1 yard |

**ASSEMBLY:** Cut the ribbon into 4 pieces, 8″ to 9″ each. Use a hand sewing needle and matching thread to sew each button to the middle of 1 length of ribbon. Trim the ends of the ribbon diagonally to prevent fraying. Tie the ribbon around a rolled or folded napkin so that the button is on top.

# appliquéd napkin rings

Simple shapes are highlighted with machine appliqué to make these perky napkin rings. Use fabric scraps or purchase ⅛-yard cuts of fabric to make the motifs. Your family and friends will appreciate receiving sets of napkin rings as gifts.

**ALL MOTIFS:** Refer to Napkin Ring Motifs on page 28. Complete Steps 1–7. Continue as described below for each motif. Then hand sew the middle of an 8″–9″ piece of the ribbon to the back of the motif. Tie the ribbon ends around a rolled napkin, letting the motif rest on top.

**DIAMOND:** Stitch around the edges of the motif in matching thread. Set the zigzag width slightly narrower. Stitch ¾″ in from the edges with contrasting thread to make the interior diamond.

**CIRCLE:** Mark or trace 4 B circles on the paper side of the fusible web. Fuse as a group to the wrong side of fabric B. Cut out each circle on the marked line. Peel off the paper backing. Fuse each circle to the front of a motif. Zigzag around the edges of each circle with contrasting thread.

**FLOWER:** Mark or trace 4 B circles on the paper side of the fusible web. Fuse as a group to the wrong side of fabric B. Cut out each circle on the marked line. Peel off the paper backing. Fuse each piece to the front of a flower motif. Zigzag the flower and petal outlines with matching thread. Zigzag around the flower center with coordinating thread.

## Materials

| FOR 4 NAPKIN RINGS | FABRIC A | FABRIC B | FAST2FUSE (4 each) | PAPER-BACKED FUSIBLE WEB | ⅜″-WIDE GROSGRAIN RIBBON |
|---|---|---|---|---|---|
| DIAMOND | ⅛ yard | n/a | 3″ × 3″ | n/a | 1 yard |
| CIRCLE | ⅛ yard | scrap | 3″ × 3″ | scrap | 1 yard |
| FLOWER | ⅛ yard | scrap | 4″ × 4″ | scrap | 1 yard |

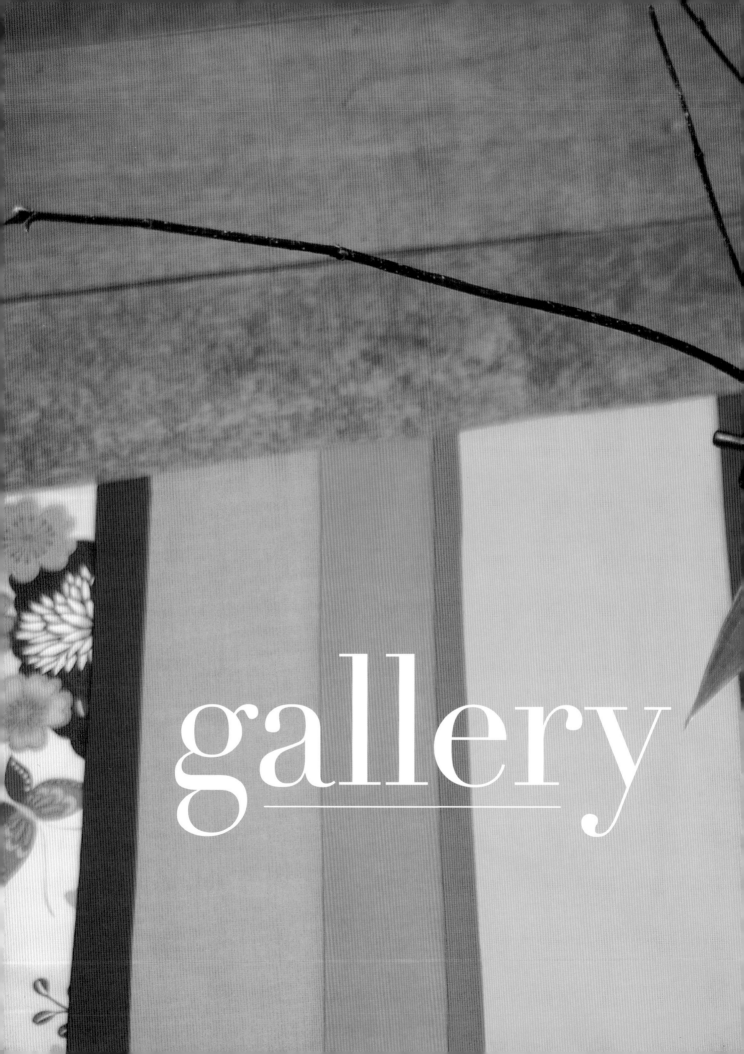

A kitschy retro print sets off our vintage greenware. The napkin's circle print is reminiscent of dress fabrics from the 1930s.

# side panels placemats

# square tablecloth

# reversible table topper

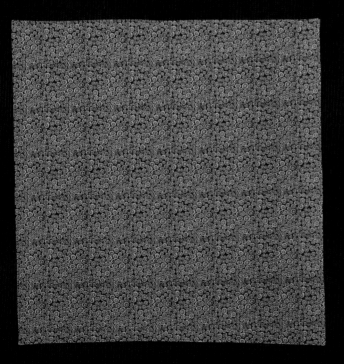

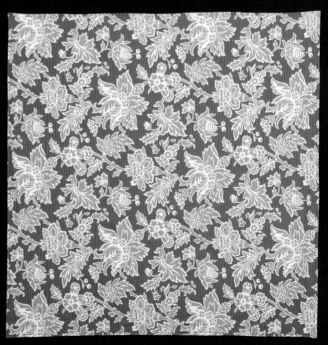

# bound edge placemat
——— & ———
## mitered corner napkins

# index

# sources

**FABRIC AND SUPPLIES**

The Stitchin' Post
P.O. Box 280
311 W. Cascade Street
Sisters, OR 97759
541-549-6061
www.stitchinpost.com

The Cotton Patch
1025 Brown Avenue, Dept. CTB
Lafayette, CA 94549
800-835-4418
www.quiltusa.com
cottonpatch@quiltusa.com

**FAST2FUSE INTERFACING**

C&T Publishing
P.O. Box 1456
Lafayette, CA 94549
800-284-1114
www.ctpub.com

**GREEN TABLE, PAGE 44**

The Wild Hare
P.O. Box 280
311 W. Cascade Street
Sisters, OR 97759
541-549-6061
www.stitchinpost.com

# ABOUT THE AUTHORS

Jean Wells and her daughter Valori Wells are a well-known duo involved in quiltmaking and fabric design, and they operate The Stitchin' Post in Sisters, Oregon.

Jean established this destination quilt shop in 1975 and has since won many awards for her business and quilting skills. She has traveled extensively, giving lectures, teaching workshops, and sharing her love of sewing with thousands of quilters worldwide. She is the founder of the annual Sisters Outdoor Quilt Show.

When Valori was in college, she and Jean began collaborating on quilting books with a garden flair. Valori's talents as a photographer captured nature at its best, and her inspirational images soon became the focus of her own distinctive quilting style. Her career came into full blossom when she began designing fabrics for the quilting industry. Valori returned to Sisters seven years ago to join her mother in managing the store. Currently she is a designer for Free Spirit Textiles.

Both women have been spreading their wings in the direction of soft furnishings. *Oh So Easy Table Toppers* is the third book in a series devoted to sewing projects for the home. Valori and her husband, Ross, recently welcomed their first child, Olivia Rose, into their family. Jean and her husband, John, live just outside Sisters, Oregon, where they have a large garden.

Also in This Series

# Great Titles
## from C&T PUBLISHING

**Indygo Junction's**
**Needle Felting**
22 Stylish Projects for Home & Fashion

**Amy Barickman**

**dimensional DELIGHTS**
20 Folding Fabric Screens to Personalize, Embellish + Display

**Liz Aneloski**

**fast fun & easy HOME ACCENTS**
**Pam Archer**
15 Fabric Projects to Decorate Any Space

**miy make it your**
Sew with Style  Easy Step-by-Step Instructions  Uniquely You
**your space**

**Shannon Mullen**

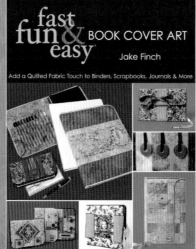

**fast fun & easy BOOK COVER ART**
**Jake Finch**
Add a Quilted Fabric Touch to Binders, Scrapbooks, Journals & More

**fast2fuse INTERFACING**  **CRAFT PACK**
Double-Sided Fusible Stiff Interfacing

**STANDARD WEIGHT STIFFNESS**
- Fusible on both sides to save you time!
- Easy to mark, cut & sew
- Perfect for fabric & paper

**USE FOR:**
- Fabric bowls, boxes & vases
- Purses, totes & bags · Kids crafts
- Art quilts · Hats & caps & more

Includes FREE PURSE pattern!